10 Minute Time Management:

The Stress-Free Guide to Getting Stuff Done

Ric Thompson

Just to say Thank You for Purchasing this Book
I want to give you a gift
100% absolutely FREE
A Copy of My Special Report "*Outsource Time*"

Go to

www.DoneForYouSolutions.com/OutsourceTime

to Receive Your FREE Gift

Table of Contents

Introduction

I want to thank you and congratulate you for purchasing, *10 Minute Time Management: The Stress-Free Guide to Getting Stuff Done.*

This book contains proven steps and strategies on how to effectively use just 10 minutes of your time to accomplish your productivity goals. Imagine what you could do with 60 hours. You could get a lot done, right? Well, if you reserve just 10 minutes every day for a year, you will have been productive for 60 hours!

So, what if you were to reserve several 10 minute productivity periods each day? Your productivity would explode! All those little annoying tasks you've been putting off for weeks or maybe even months would get done, and you would still have energy after completing them. So much energy, in fact, that you might even dedicate more than 10 minutes to finishing your work.

While it might not seem like a lot of time, you can get things *done* in 10 minutes. In fact, 10 minute time management is a procrastinator's dream. Why? It's because you can do anything for ten minutes. Your brain knows that 10 minutes is doable for any task, pleasant or not. When you know you can stop working on a task after 10 minutes, you are more likely to buckle down and work for that amount of time.

Of course, you can't be productive if you aren't ready for those 10 minutes. This guide will also help you get ready to make your 10 minutes the most effective they can be. It will teach you to use your spare minutes wisely to accomplish even more of your productivity goals.

Sometimes, it can be difficult to tackle a huge project because you know it's going to take up a lot of your time.

However, using these 10 minute time management tips and strategies will help you break down those larger tasks into manageable chunks. You will be amazed at how much you get done and how much less stress you have by budgeting your time in 10 minute increments.

By purchasing this book, you have taken a giant step toward meeting your productivity goals without the high levels of stress that often come with deadlines and difficult projects.

Thanks again for purchasing, I hope you enjoy it!

Ric Thompson

Make a Daily Plan

First things first: you simply cannot be productive if you do not know what you want to accomplish. This is why it is critical for you to create a plan that you can flawlessly execute when your 10 minute productivity period rolls around. A plan also helps you avoid procrastination and prevents you from spending your 10 minutes on organization.

The way in which your daily plan takes shape will depend on your style. Perhaps you like to write everything down in a day planner to help you keep track of everything you have to do. Or maybe you prefer an online to-do list that allows you to access it from any computer. It doesn't really matter how or where you keep your plan as long as you are able to access it easily and quickly when your 10 minute productivity period begins.

Once you have your format for your daily plan you can begin to get organized. However, you don't want to spend more than 10 minutes on this aspect of productivity either – the object here is productivity, not busy work. Set a timer before you start listing the tasks you want to work on for the day. This will keep you from spending too much time on your plan. Remember, the goal is to get you to be productive in chunks, so make your goals realistic. Don't write down that you are going to "balance the books" if you haven't opened QuickBooks once in the past 6 months. It just isn't going to happen.

Instead, focus on small tasks that will eventually add up to bigger projects. For example, if your eventual goal is to get the books balanced, your initial task can be downloading and categorizing the bank transactions for the first month. You will be amazed at how many of those smaller tasks you can get done in just 10 minutes every day! They really add up and before long, you will see how much better you can manage your bookkeeping tasks.

Creating the Plan

The first step toward developing your daily plan is to determine how many 10 minute productivity periods you want to include in your day. For some people, a single session per day is all they can devote to time management, at least at first. Certainly, that is better than doing nothing to move toward your goals, but if you can dedicate two or three 10-minute sessions each day to productivity, you are going to accomplish your bigger goals much sooner.

Owning your own business requires you to meet deadlines. You might have to set 10 minutes each hour or every other hour that you devote your whole attention to a project. In this scenario, you won't be able to just set one 10 minute session per day and expect to meet your deadlines. Effective time management is all about budgeting your time so that you aren't scrambling at the last minute to complete a task that could have easily been completed without stress if it had been broken down into smaller tasks.

Once you decide how many 10 minute productivity periods you are going to have during the day, it's time to decide what you are going to do during each session. Again, you don't want to spend any of your 10 minutes trying to decide what to do. Before you know it, the 10 minutes will be gone and you won't be any closer to your goal.

Be sure to keep your tasks realistic so you can get them done in your 10 minutes. However, that doesn't mean you have to finish your task completely. This might sound contradictory, but you can "finish" what you intended to accomplish in your 10 minutes without finishing the entire task. For instance, if you have a huge project that needs to be completed within two weeks, you aren't going to finish it in 10 minutes. However, you can finish a specific part of the job in 10 minutes. That is what you should focus on.

If you have multiple projects you need to work on, you may have to set multiple 10 minute sessions to accomplish a little portion of each project. This is a great strategy for productivity because it allows you to work on a variety of tasks without getting burnt out by trying to push through and complete just one. The old saying is that variety is the spice of life, and it certainly applies to time management. You will get more done if you divide your tasks into smaller increments and spend time on each task every day.

Plan Your Day in Just 10 Minutes

When your time is up, stop planning. During your 10 minute planning session, you will have generated plenty of tasks to accomplish throughout your day. You don't want to overwhelm yourself with a hundred little things you want to cross off your list before you go to bed. Over-planning causes stress and the whole point of dividing your work up into smaller chunks is to reduce the amount of stress you feel when confronted with demands on your time.

You will find that as you get more experienced with making a daily plan, you will cherish the 10 minutes you spend planning your productivity sessions. You might even look forward to your productivity periods because you know how much you are going to get done during that time. You will learn what tasks you can complete in 10 minutes and which ones need to be broken down even more.

The key to making your daily plan effective is to ensure you have scheduled your 10 minute sessions and have actually blocked out that time so that nothing will get in your way of keeping those commitments. You should schedule your sessions just as you would a doctor's appointment or important meeting. You don't want to push these sessions off because that will defeat the entire purpose of 10 minute time management. Nothing is going to happen during those 10 minutes that can't be addressed in minute 11.

That being said, there will be times when you may have to reschedule a productivity period or two. Just be sure that you do reschedule it and keep your session whenever you can. Your productivity depends on it.

Organization

Initially, you are probably going to have to spend some of your 10-minute productivity periods getting organized. This is because you can't be productive if you are always looking for your materials and tools you need to complete a project. In addition, you don't want to spend any part of your 10 minute productivity sessions gathering supplies. They should be ready for you the moment you set your alarm and begin work.

During your first 10 minute productivity period, decide what you are going to need to tackle your first project. Are you doing the month-end books for your business? Make sure you have all the applicable forms up on your computer so they are ready to go when you are. Are you writing this month's newsletter? Gather all information you are going to include in the newsletter before you start. Open the application you use to write it and keep it minimized on your computer until your productivity period begins.

If you need a workspace for your project, use a 10 minute productivity period to create it. Perhaps you are preparing a marketing campaign and you need space to create your presentation materials. Take 10 minutes to get your area ready for work. This way, when your 10 minute session rolls around, you don't have to spend time getting the space ready.

Organization Tips

After the first few organizing sessions, you don't want to spend too many of them organizing and preparing for your productivity periods. You will want to develop systems to keep your organized as you go. You may not realize it, but you lose a huge amount of time every week and possibly every day looking for things you can't find because you aren't organized. Here are some tips to help you get your workspace organized to boost your productivity.

1. **Only keep essentials on your workspace.** Remove everything else that might distract you from meeting your productivity goals.

2. **Supplies should be within easy reach of your workspace**. You don't want to waste time getting up to find a pen or digging through a drawer to locate notecards.

3. **Place a trash can near your workspace.** You are probably going to generate trash during your sessions. You will want an easy place to toss it so you don't make more work for yourself later.

4. **Purchase containers that can help you stay organized**. For example, store papers in files, notebooks or large envelopes. Get a pencil holder for pens and pencils. Group like items together and put them in storage containers. Be sure to label all containers to make sure you can find your supplies when you need them. Try not to add items you know you won't use or you aren't sure what you will use them for. This just adds clutter and can actually increase the amount of stress you have.

5. **Divide up your workspace into categories like the reference area, the supply area and the work area.** This will enable you to keep your work area clutter free in addition to having everything you need at your fingertips.

6. **Keep a notebook nearby or create a file you keep open on your computer to jot down tasks you want to add to your 10 minute productivity sessions later on.**

7. **Bookmark your favorite websites.** Whether on your computer or your tablet, use the bookmark function so you can find the websites you use most frequently at the touch of a button.

8. **Organize your computer files.** When you have to search for a file, you are wasting precious time. Your filing system should be basic and simple to understand. Also, be sure to use the search function when looking for a file. This will result in less work for you because the computer can find the file you want in an instant.

9. **Keep all your passwords in one place.** As you likely know, almost every website requires a username and password to access certain information. It's very difficult for anyone to remember all of the various passwords for every account ever created. In addition, if you haven't visited a site for a while, it's very possible you have forgotten your username, password or both. It is aggravating when you have to use the password lookup feature on the website because you usually have to wait at least a few minutes for it to be delivered to you via email. A program like

Roboform can help you keep all of your passwords in one secure place. You can also access your passwords from any device so you aren't tied down to just one if you need to get business done elsewhere.

It won't take you long to establish a routine for your major work spaces in your home or office. You should only spend one or two 10 minute productivity periods organizing each work space to the point where you can be productive during later sessions. If you find you need more time to get your workspace ready, take it, but keep in mind that your goal is to become more productive each day. While organizing your tools and supplies is an important step toward 10 minute time management, it's only one of the steps you need to take.

Preparation = Less Stress

Getting your workspace organized will also reduce the amount of stress you are under to get things done. Much of the stress you experience related to time management is comes from feeling out of control. When you are organized, you are essentially retaking control of at least one aspect of your life. When you are prepared, you know exactly what to expect. When you know exactly what to expect, you won't stress over the unknown.

People naturally fear what they don't know. While some people can thrive in chaotic situations, most people don't. Sometimes, they even shut down completely, making them even less productive than before. Even if your desk is slightly cluttered, it can cause stress, even if you don't realize it. Your attention is not focused completely on the task at hand. A part of your brain is thinking about what to do about that clutter. You might be somewhat productive during that time, but you aren't going to be as productive as you want to be.

As you are organizing your workspace, think about how the space is arranged. You don't have to rearrange furniture or other items right away, but it might be a task you want to add to your list down the road. You want your room arrangement to be healthy, comfortable and convenient. For instance, don't put your printer all the way across the room. You don't want to spend part of your precious time walking to the printer to get your printouts. If you get distracted by a window right across from your desk, consider turning your desk around so you face away from the window.

Remember that you don't need to accomplish all of these organization ideas at once. Use several 10 minute productivity periods to accomplish them incrementally. Over time, you will realize how much more you get done in with an organized workspace.

Deadlines

Some tasks don't require deadlines. They just end when they end. However, most tasks, especially those related to business have deadlines that must be met. Part of learning how to manage your time better is knowing how to set deadlines and budget your time effectively so that those deadlines are consistently met.

You might think the word "deadline" has a negative connotation, particularly if you are constantly under pressure to meet short deadlines. When you feel like you don't have enough time to get something done, your stress level skyrockets. Unfortunately, if you don't set deadlines, you may not get anything done at all. Procrastinators are notoriously prone to waiting until the last minute to get things done. If there isn't a deadline, then there isn't a "last minute." They can keep pushing their tasks off indefinitely.

To begin the process of setting deadlines, you must first learn to look at deadlines in a new way. They are not torture devices devised by the Evil God of the Entrepreneurs to stress you out. They are actually very useful in helping you manage your time and become more productive on a daily basis.

If you are facing external deadlines, set by someone other than yourself, a client perhaps, you will have to be very careful when you budget your time to make sure you meet the demands of the job. If you are the one imposing the deadlines, you can work at a pace you are comfortable with as long as you are meeting your own needs. In either case, though, you must make sure you set deadlines that are both realistic and achievable.

Why Do You Need Deadlines?

Deadlines aren't just useful in helping you budget your time. They are also beneficial in a number of other ways, including:

1. **Continuously moving you toward your goals**. Setting multiple deadlines on your way to accomplishing the ultimate goal can help you see the progress you are making toward the finish line.

2. **Providing you with a sense of accomplishment.** Meeting or even beating your deadlines can fill you with pride and give you the incentive you need to continue to meet other deadlines. There is no better feeling than crossing an item off your to do list.

3. **Helping stave off procrastination.** Without deadlines, it can be tempting to put off difficult or unpleasant tasks. Deadlines force you to get stuff done, even if you don't want to.

4. **Preventing you from overloading your schedule.** Of course, you can't always control the deadlines imposed on you by others (namely, bosses), you can avoid taking on more than you can handle by knowing when your current deadlines are. For instance, if you know you have a big project due on the 18th, you probably won't commit yourself to making cupcakes for the PTA's bake sale the night before.

Make Your Deadlines Realistic

Now comes the hard part. If you are setting your own deadlines, how do you know they are realistic and achievable? You definitely don't want to underestimate the scale of your project, setting you up for a very stressful few days or even weeks as the deadline closes in. Keep in mind that your goal is to reduce the amount of stress you are under by effectively managing your time.

One rule of thumb you should use when setting deadlines for yourself is to carefully consider how much time you expect the entire project to take and multiple that number by 1.5. For example, if you think your project is going to take 10 days to complete, plan to give yourself 15 days. This will allow you some wiggle room in case you are not as productive as you thought you would be. Setting an earlier final deadline will not only reduce your stress level by allowing you more time, but it will also be extremely satisfying when you finish earlier.

Once you set your final deadline, it's time to budget your 10 minute productivity periods so that you can accomplish your goal. Now, setting these 10 minute deadlines will depend on how many total hours you allot for the project. If you believe the project is going to take 40 hours to complete, you will need to have multiple 10 minute sessions to complete your job. Certainly, one 10 minute productivity period per day is not going to move you close to your goal unless your deadline is way out in the future.

Here's where a series of 10 minute productivity sessions may not be enough to meet your deadline. However, you still need to use this strategy for portions of your project that require intense focus. Save the parts of your project that are going to demand all of your attention for your 10 minute productivity periods. You will have to work on this project at other times during your day, but setting aside 10 minutes every day or every morning and afternoon to concentrate on what you need to get done that day can be more productive than spending several hours giving it only part of your attention.

Remember that you can use a 10 minute session to set your deadlines, as this is a critical component to your project. Don't be afraid to sit down and map out the entire project before you actually start so that you don't get sidetracked along the way. This is an excellent use of your time and will make you more productive as you go on. As you plan your 10 minute sessions, carefully consider what you want to accomplish during that time. Don't try to do too much or you will just get frustrated. These mini deadlines will add up and move you closer to your final deadline.

Deadlines can seem impossible to meet, especially if you don't break them up into more manageable pieces. You don't want to add more stress to your life by looking at the only the final deadline. 10 minute chunks of productivity can help you view your deadlines in a more positive way, resulting in less stress and a feeling of actually having more time than you thought because you are using it so much better.

Distractions

Technology brings with it many different tools to help you manage your time better. There are online calendars, automatic reminders, checklist templates and smartphones with the capability of managing your entire life. These are wonderful tools and really can make a difference in how you spend your time. Unfortunately, these same tools can provide distractions that prevent you from using your time wisely.

In just 10 minutes or less, you can eliminate these distractions so that when you work, your attention can be entirely focused on getting things done. It's not easy to ignore distractions that come with today's ever connected world of business, but with a little self-discipline, you can set yourself up to succeed. Follow these steps to accomplish this goal.

1. **Identify your distractions**. Take a couple of minutes to think objectively about what distracts you from getting tasks done. Is it your phone? Your email? Twitter? Facebook? Whatever they are, write them down so you can consider solutions.

2. **Take steps to remove distractions from your workspace.** Some distractions can't be removed entirely, such as a landline phone, but others don't even need to be in your workspace during your 10 minute productivity sessions. For instance, make your workspace a cell phone-free zone. Leave it in another room, if it's one of your distractions. You won't be as tempted to answer it if it rings or play a game or check your fantasy football scores.

3. **Establish a set time in the morning and afternoon when you will check your email and respond to them**. In most cases, you can use a 10 minute productivity period to check your email. You might need a second one to respond, but the point is, you do not need to check your email every few minutes. Most people expect you to respond to an email within 24 hours, so designating a time in the morning and afternoon will allow you to meet those expectations.

4. **The same goes for social media and online blogs**. Facebook and Twitter are two of the biggest time suckers on the planet. Once you start reading the posts, it's very difficult to stop. You could find that hours pass before you know it and you've wasted so much time that you are now rushing around to meet your deadlines. Rushing equals stress, so social media can actually cause stress if you don't manage the time you spend on it. Don't keep the icons pinned to your tool bars. That makes it too tempting to click. Blogs can also suck your time away from you by drawing you into the first one and enticing you to keep reading by suggesting other posts or blogs you might enjoy. The Internet is full of material that can get you completely off track in your quest to manage your time better.

5. **Develop a "no visitors" policy when you are working during your 10 minute productivity period**. If you are in an office, talk to your coworkers about your plan to work on a project for a solid 10 minutes without interruption. If you are at home, close the door to your workspace and put a "do not disturb" sign on the door. You should also let your family know you are working for 10 minutes and that you will be out when the timer sounds. This sets guidelines for you and your family members to allow you to be the most productive you can be.

6. **Turn off the ringer on your landline telephone.** You can make your workspace a cell-phone free zone, but your landline is another story. It likely has to stay in your workspace and can become a huge distraction if you let it. You might see who is calling and decide to put off your 10-minute productivity period until after you speak to the caller. Before you know it, your 30 second conversation has turned into an hour-long chat. Most of your phone calls can wait until your dedicated work time is over. They will leave a message or call back.

7. **Check your workspace for other distractions that might not be apparent to you.** Can you work with noise? If not, try to eliminate any noises that could keep you from being productive. Do you tend to stare out the window? If so, try moving your desk to where you are not able to look out of it without getting up.

8. **Do not use your computer for your work if it's not absolutely necessary.** The computer is an excellent tool, but it is also a minefield for distraction as well. Of course, if you're an entrepreneur, you probably use your computer for everything, so not using it isn't even an option. However, you can minimize the distractions on your computer by shutting down browsers if you're working offline or closing social media and email tabs if you are working online. Even if you promise yourself you won't look at email or check your Facebook page, it's a lot more tempting to do it anyway if your computer is right there. You say, "I'll just take a quick break," but you might not come back. You shouldn't take any breaks during your 10 minute productivity periods because it's just 10 minutes. Any deviation from you plan will translate to a loss of productivity.

You are likely going to come across other distractions as you set your schedule and start making 10 minute time management a priority in your life. Your job is to deal with them in a manner that allows you to continue your productivity. Try to work through the distraction when you first come across it so your 10 minute session is completed, but take care of it as soon as you can afterward. Most distractions have easy solutions, but some might take some additional thought.

Distractions can really derail your time management plan. They can prevent you from reaching your goals and allow you to fall back into your old habits and patterns. You might say, "I'll only check my email this once," but it's a slippery slope that is difficult to climb back up. Remove as many distractions as you can while you are working so you can develop new habits that are in line with your time management goals.

Delegate

One of the best ways to manage your time is to assign tasks that can be done by someone else *to* someone else. Your time is better spent when you can focus on those tasks that only you can do. This strategy is not very complicated and can be done in 10 minutes or less. It is effective in a business setting and a home setting, provided you have other people you can delegate tasks to.

Some people might think it's easier to do everything themselves rather than spend time divvying up the tasks and following up on their completion. However, your ultimate goal is to free up time to do the tasks on your priority list that no one else can do for you. This includes activities like:

1. Building your business by bringing in new clients.
2. Reflecting on business practices to identify areas of improvement.
3. Planning (your day, your meeting, your vacation).
4. Building stronger relationships with current clients and customers.
5. Researching new business practices and learning how to implement them.
6. Taking personal development classes.
7. Creating a better work-home balance.
8. Doing something just for fun.

The concept of delegation is really very simple. You choose one or more tasks on your to-do list and you give it to someone else (an outsourcer, your spouse, a child) who can also do the task up to your expectations. In reality, though, delegating can be difficult because it may appear to the person getting the task that you are not taking care of your responsibilities. You also need to make sure everyone is clear about who is doing what so that nothing falls through the cracks. This requires some oversight on your part, but if you delegate properly, the time you spend on these tasks can be greatly reduced.

The Delegation Process

Again, as with other time management techniques, you don't want to spend a lot of time putting them into practice. You can delegate quite a few tasks on your to-do list to other people and you can do it within 10 minutes, if you have a system in place. Here are the steps to effective delegation.

1. **Identify the tasks on your to-do list that someone else can do.** You may have to set your ego aside and get past the idea that if you want something done right you have to do it yourself. You are not the only person who can do these tasks and you might even discover someone else can to them better, especially if they have the time to do them right.

2. **Don't wait for a volunteer.** Your kids aren't going to volunteer to clean the bathroom and your VA isn't going to volunteer to do the research for that proposal she doesn't know anything about. It just isn't going to happen. Ultimately, you have to tell people what you need. It's your job to communicate with your family, outsourcers, or employees what they can do to help you.

3. **Identify people who are capable of completing the tasks up to your expectations**. If you can't come up with anyone who you trust enough to let him or her take over some of your responsibilities, you're going to have to train someone. This way, you will teach that person exactly what you want the results of the task to be. Training the right person to take over these tasks is a long-term investment to better time management for you. You will save time in the long run when you don't have to correct mistakes or end up doing the task yourself anyway.

4. **Gather the materials and resources your delegate is going to need to be successful**. Before you ask someone to take over a portion of your to-do list, you should have everything he or she will need to perform the task up to your standards. Don't expect him or her to have everything on hand, or to be able to read your mind and know how you want it done. Your task will be completed more quickly if your person doesn't have to flounder around trying to figure things out. For example, if you ask your VA to handle your customer service emails, make sure you have the common questions and their responses in a knowledgebase or a training document for him or her to get started right away.

5. **Prepare yourself to ask the person to take over a task.** Call him or her on the phone and ask directly or send an email asking for a response by a specific date. It's okay for him or her to think your request over before providing a response, but you need to let it be known that you need to hear back as quickly as possible so you can make other arrangements if necessary.

6. **Ask the person to take over the task.** Explain why you need help and tell him or her that you do not care how the job gets done as long as it gets done to your expectations. This is the critical component of effective delegation. Your assistant might not approach the task in the same way you would. Understand that it doesn't really matter how it is approached if your objective is accomplished. You can show the person how you do it, but don't expect him or her to do it exactly the same way you do. If you allow your person to develop his or her own technique, he or she is more likely to do a good job on the task. No one likes to be micromanaged. Your people are intelligent human beings who may even be able to improve on your process if given the ownership of the task and the latitude to do so.

All of the six delegation steps mentioned here can be done in 10 minutes or less and can make a huge impact on your time. You will be surprised at how much more you can accomplish when you trust other people to do some of the tasks you don't need to do yourself.

Use Downtime Wisely

Downtime is the bane of people who do not know how to manage their time well. For example, if you have ten minutes before you need to leave for your next meeting, you might think you don't have time to do anything, so you do nothing. This is not a good use of your time. As shown throughout this book, you can get a lot done in ten minutes, even if you don't plan ahead of time.

You experience many periods of downtime throughout your day. 10 minutes here, five minutes there. You don't really think about these brief periods of time as a waste, but if you add them all up, they really are. You are unproductive during your downtime if you use it in ways that are not moving you toward your goals. Just as you could potentially add 60 hours of productivity each year by dedicating one 10 minute session to focusing on a task every day, you can lose 60 hours of productivity each year by allowing one 10 minute time block go by without getting something done each day.

Now this doesn't mean you shouldn't take breaks once in a while. You definitely should. You don't want to get burned out by filling your days with task after task without taking time out to enjoy life. However, if your main complaint is that you do not have enough time in your day to get everything done that needs to be done, you will want to take advantage of those times when you appear to have nothing to do.

Transform Your Commute

One of the biggest time suckers for most people is their commute. They drive to and from an office every day, which really cuts into their productivity. If this describes you, then you have two choices: you can work closer to your home (or IN it in some cases) or you can learn to use your commute more effectively. If you're reading this, then it's likely you have chosen the second option.

Technology has progressed to the point where you can conduct business while on the go without compromising your driving ability. Here are some of the ways you can spend your driving downtime to make it more productive and move you toward your goals.

1. **Listen to an audiobook**. There are hundreds of books that can help you improve in any area of life you choose. Most of these books are available in audio format. Use your drive time to listen to these books. Even if you don't end up using the techniques in a book, you are still exposing yourself to new ideas and potential improvements that can benefit you in the long run. If self-improvement books aren't your style, listen to a book for entertainment purposes instead. You might think you don't have time to read, but doing it while you are driving is a great way to fit it in.

2. **Work the phone**. Cell phones have made driving while talking a common occurrence, but rather than use that time to chat with a friend, use it instead to schedule appointments, check your bank account balances, follow up with a client, listen to your voicemail and register your kids for various activities. Certainly, you should only use a hands-

free device to make these calls and you will have to have the information you need to complete the phone tasks with you, but this can be an excellent time to work the phone if you don't want to use up your precious time at home or the office.

3. **Brainstorm**. Many people don't take the time to come up with various ways to approach a problem. The brainstorming phase of problem solving is usually cut short because more time is needed on actually solving the problem. However, brainstorming often leads to more creative and effective ways to solve problems rather than continuing to do things the way they have always been done. Some people can't brainstorm without writing their ideas down, which isn't advisable if you're driving. Instead, use a small digital recorder to capture your thoughts.

4. **Write emails and other communications**. Of course, you don't want to actually write emails when you are driving. That would be a definite hazard. Instead, use software designed to type what you speak into an application like your email program or Microsoft Word. A wonderful program that can help you do this is <u>Dragon Naturally Speaking</u>. This software is easy to use, affordable and very accurate. <u>The Speak It! Text to Speech</u> app is an excellent choice if you want to work on your smartphone or tablet. It is available on iTunes and the Google App Store. If you have a laptop, bring it with you along with a hands-free microphone connected to your computer. Then, while you're driving, you can dictate emails, letters or blog posts that you can send or post later. You will want to proofread and edit your writings

before you send them out because even though the software is pretty accurate, there will probably still be some mistakes you will want to correct.

5. **Exercise.** Yes, you can fit a little bit of exercise in your day while you are driving. You won't be able to do aerobics or anything vigorous, but you can simulate lifting weights, which will strengthen your muscles and burn some fat. Dynamic strength exercises work by contracting your muscles and mimicking the action of lifting weights. You can work out your biceps, triceps, shoulders and abs while you drive using this technique. This website gives some great advice on how to work out in your car. You can also get some extra tips in the book *1-Minute Isometrics – Build Strength in One Minute*. While it isn't necessarily a substitute for working out in the more traditional sense, it can move you closer to your fitness goals if that's the only time you have during the day to exercise.

Make Wait Time Work Time

Another way you can sneak in 10 minutes of productivity is to take advantage of waiting. Think about how often you are waiting for something. You wait to see your doctor. You wait in the parking lot for your children to get out of school. You wait for clients. You wait in line. You wait on hold. Waiting has become a way of life. This time can be wasted or it can be productive, depending on how you use it.

Imagine that you arrive at your kids' school 10 minutes before the bell rings. You can sit in your car listening to the radio, which probably isn't a very productive activity, or you can organize that file you've been meaning to get to. Maybe you need to plan your spouse's birthday party or schedule the carpet cleaners. Whatever it is you've been putting off because you don't have time due to your other responsibilities, you can probably get it done while you wait for the bell to ring. Even if you don't get the entire task done, you will have made a dent in it, meaning there will be less for you to do later.

Waiting to see your doctor can be aggravating, especially if he or she is running late (is there any other way). Rather than get upset, be prepared with tasks you can work on while you are waiting. Plan your week or write down your grocery list. If you're seeing the doctor because of a health concern, use the time you have to generate a list of questions you want to ask him or her when you finally get seen. This will save time during the exam.

Bring your laptop or tablet with you to your appointment so you can compose emails, respond to messages or research your next project. It isn't advised that you return calls while in the waiting room, but you can listen to your voicemail and make a list of who you need to call back later. You can also spend the time planning for a meeting, presentation or other upcoming situation you need time to address.

Productive people use their downtime effectively because they know the minutes add up to hours. You will never get that time back, so take advantage of it when it is available to you. Even if you're not able to work on a task that has been identified as a priority during your downtime, you can still make headway on the various other tasks that keep getting pushed to the end of the list. You will be amazed at how much you can accomplish by being prepared to get things done whenever you have a few spare minutes.

Reward Yourself

Even the most productive person on the planet needs an incentive to use his or her time effectively. Often, that incentive is money. When you are expected to complete tasks for your clients, you do them. Many times, you are probably able to use your time effectively because you know your income depends on it. However, as a self-employed business owner, you also know how easy it can be to put off tasks until the last minute, since there is no one telling you what to do.

As a business owner, you are in charge of managing your own time rather than having a boss to do it for you, it can be challenging to find the time to get everything done. You've already learned that setting aside 10 minutes to direct your entire focus on one specific task can help you reach your goals. However, you might be finding it hard to stick to your plan.

Perhaps you can't get away from your distractions, even though you've tried to eliminate them. Or you discover you're behind schedule and you need to skip your 10 minute productivity period to get caught up (even though skipping it will actually get you further behind). In these cases, you need a little extra incentive to work solidly on a task for 10 minutes. A reward, given to yourself when the timer signals 10 minutes have passed can go a long way in getting you to commit to 10 minute time management.

Small Rewards Pay Big Dividends

Everyone likes to get a reward, even if it's a small reward that might not be an incentive to anyone but you. Certainly, you aren't going to reward yourself with a beach vacation for sticking to your 10 minute time management strategy, but perhaps you like playing a particular game on your phone, or getting a latte and you use that as an incentive to push through your 10 minute productivity session. Be sure not to play more than one game, or get a latte for every successfully completed 10 minute period though, or you venture into the time-wasting (and waist expanding) arena.

You should always recognize your accomplishments, even if they are small in comparison to your overarching goal. When you make progress toward that goal it is an occasion to celebrate. Your celebration should be proportionate to the accomplishment, so allowing yourself to check your Facebook page after completing a 10 minute task would be entirely appropriate.

Giving yourself breaks is another way to reward yourself for all your hard work. You can't work continuously without taking a break now and then. Your brain needs it and your body needs it. You will be better able to focus on your task at hand if you know you have a break coming up in 10 minutes. You can do anything for 10 minutes, especially if you are rewarded afterward.

As you get used to building these 10 minute productivity session into your schedule, you might find you don't need as many rewards for getting things done. You may discover the feeling of accomplishment is its own reward, which is partly what you wanted when you decided to learn how to manage your time better. There is no better feeling than crossing items off your to-do list, especially if they have been on there for quite some time. In fact, some people put tasks on their list just so they can have the satisfaction of crossing them off when they complete them. Productivity is actually its own reward, but it might take you a little while to learn that, so giving yourself a different kind of reward now and then for meeting a goal is a great way to get you to that point.

Consider this for a minute: when you tell your children to clean their room before they can go to the movies with a friend, you are rewarding them for working hard to reach their goal. When you tell them to do their homework before turning on the television, you are giving them an incentive to complete an unpleasant task before getting a reward. You do it all the time with your kids, so why don't you do it for yourself? You deserve rewards for working hard. Many companies give their employees incentives to meet the organization's goals, but if you work for yourself, *you* have to provide those rewards yourself.

Reward Suggestions

Here are some excellent small-scale rewards you can give yourself when you complete a successful 10-minute productivity session:

1. Your favorite latte at Starbucks.

2. 10 minutes to read a book for pleasure.

3. A walk outside.

4. Play time with your kids or pets.

5. 10 minutes to watch a recorded program (so you can pause it and pick up where you left off later).

6. 10 minutes to listen to your favorite songs on your iPod.

7. A special treat (ice cream, smoothie, candy, soda etc.)

8. Give yourself points for each 10 minute session and save up your points for a larger reward.

9. 10 minutes for a power nap (be careful with this one. You don't want to end up taking a two-hour nap and losing ground on your goals).

10. 10 minutes to play a computer game.

The key to rewarding yourself appropriately is to keep the reward proportionate to the accomplishment. Don't allow yourself to read for the rest of the afternoon just because you worked non-stop on a project for 10 minutes. As with anything, you need to exercise self-control when rewarding yourself. It should be used as an incentive to work hard, but not as an excuse to get out of working more.

Be careful to only reward yourself if you deserve it. If you wouldn't let your kids go to the movies if only half their room is clean, then don't give yourself a reward if you don't meet your goal. Save it for another time and get yourself back on track. Rewards are meaningless if you haven't earned them, even if you're the only one who knows you didn't meet your goal.

Keep your rewards small (about 10 minutes in time or less) and try to increase the amount of work you need to complete before getting a reward as you get better at managing your time. You will discover the feeling you get when you accomplish your goals is better than any other reward you might receive.

Learn to Say No

If you are looking for the fastest time management strategy of all, here's one that you can do in just seconds: say no. One of the biggest reasons why people have too much on their plate and not enough to time to do it all is because they have a hard time saying no to people who want them to take on even more. You might be one of those people if you find yourself volunteering too much or being the one everyone else turns to when they need help.

These requests can really wreak havoc with your own schedule and can cause you to put off tasks that are really important to you because you are working on things that are important to other people. Of course, if it's a client asking you to take on more responsibilities, you might feel like you can't say no, since your income depends on keeping your clients happy. However, you should be able to talk to your client and work together to keep your workload manageable.

Why Can't You Say No?

Unfortunately, saying no is not as easy as it sounds, as you probably already know. In fact, you might be so uncomfortable saying no that you find yourself taking on more and more to the detriment of your own goals. There are many reasons why it's difficult to say no, including:

1. **You truly want to help**. You think people wouldn't ask you to do something if they didn't really need your help. You don't want to leave anyone in a lurch, so you agree to help out, even if your time is compromised.

2. **You are afraid of conflict.** You may think the person will take your "no" personally and confront you, so you say "yes" to keep the peace.

3. **You don't want to be known as disagreeable.** You may believe that if you say no too often, you will get a bad reputation.

4. **You fear you may miss out on a lost opportunity.** You might believe you have to take on as much as possible so you can get ahead in your business. If you say no, you may worry that you will miss the opportunity to gain a new client or to keep the clients you already have.

5. **You fear the loss of a relationship.** Since some people can take the word "no" as a personal rejection, you may be concerned you will lose a client or friend if you don't say yes.

It is very important that you get past these fears if you want to learn how to properly manage your time. Most of these fears are unfounded, as people tend to move on pretty quickly to alternative solutions. They usually understand that you are busy and will either do the task themselves or find another person who has less on his or her plate.

Saying No the Polite Way

Regardless, you have to learn how to say no the right way so that your fears don't come true. It takes practice, but eventually, you will be able to say no without worrying about the consequences, because after all, they really are all in your mind. Here are some easy ways to say no without alienating anyone.

1. **Tell the person that you are unable to commit to his or her request as you have other priorities at the moment.** This is probably the easiest way to say no because it lets the person know you have a lot going on and to hold off on other requests for a while. You can also let the person know what you are working on if you need him or her to understand the situation better.

2. **Tell the person you are right in the middle of something and ask if you can discuss the request at a later time**. This is a way to temporarily hold off the request, but it conveys the idea that you are willing to help later, when you have more time.

3. **Tell the person you would love to help, but . . .**This is a polite way of saying no to people who are looking to collaborate with you or would like you to attend a conference with them. You are telling them their ideas are excellent, but you are unable to participate because of other commitments or different priorities.

4. **Tell the person you will think about it and get back to him or her**. This is not exactly a no, but if you are interested in the request and you just aren't sure whether or not you're going to have time, this is a great way to give you some time to think it over before you commit. If the person really wants your help, he or she will be willing to wait a little while for you to make a decision. Tell him or her that you will provide an answer within a specific time frame. If you are not really interested in helping out with the task, do not use this strategy, as it will only lead him or her on.

5. **Tell the person you have different priorities at the moment, but you will keep him or her in mind for future opportunities**. This is an excellent way to say no without closing the door to working with the person in the future.

6. **Tell the person you're not the best person for the job**. If you know someone who might be willing to take on the task who can handle it better than you, give him or her a referral to that person.

7. **Just say no**. This is the most direct way to decline a task, and it is effective. As long as you say it politely, you don't have to elaborate on the reason why you can't. The person may be disappointed, but a mentioned earlier, he or she will find another solution.

Be sure to stand firm with your "no." Some people might try to convince you the task will only take a few minutes of your time, but if you cave in, you are telling this person its okay to pressure you into doing things you really don't want to do. Most people will back off when you tell them you are already committed to other tasks, but there are those who will continue to pressure you until you give in. Don't allow them to do this. Set clear boundaries and stick with them.

If you come across a request that you really want to do, but you are already committed to other projects, you may have to re-prioritize your current obligations to fit it in. However, just be careful that you don't neglect something you have committed to so you can take on the new task. This can cause serious harm to your time management plan and can interfere with accomplishing your goals.

Common Mistakes

By now you have learned many time management strategies, techniques and skills that you can do in 10 minutes or less to help you meet your goals. You have learned to use your time more wisely, even your downtime so that you aren't letting any time go to waste. You have learned the quickest time management strategy by learning how to say no. You are well prepared to start planning your 10 minute productivity sessions and get your life under control.

Still, you need to be careful about falling into some of the time management traps that can throw you off your plan. Even with the best of intentions, you can still make some common time management mistakes that can suck away your time and put you right back in the position you were in before you started reading this book. Knowing some of these mistakes ahead of time can help you avoid them.

1. **Multitasking during your 10 minute productivity sessions.** The goal of using 10 minutes to focus on a single task is to make significant progress on a project you would otherwise put on the back burner due to other pressing priorities. If you use that 10 minutes to do other things while working on the designated task, you aren't making the same amount of progress as you would by following your plan.

2. **Not getting enough sleep.** Part of the reason you are trying to manage your time better is to have more time to do the things you want to do or need to do to stay healthy. When you don't get enough sleep or the sleep you are getting isn't of the quality you need to perform at your best, you are more likely to use your time ineffectively. You may be

too tired to focus on a task for even 10 full minutes. Use some of the time you save by implementing these 10 minute time management strategies to get a few extra winks at night. You will probably even find the quality of your sleep improves because you will be less stressed when you manage your time properly.

3. **Using too much time to plan**. Many people get stuck in the planning phase and never actually execute their plans. Remember that when you plan your day, don't use more than 10 minutes. You can easily make a list of tasks you want to complete during your productivity sessions in that amount of time.

4. **Not writing tasks down**. When you plan, it is critical that you write your tasks and goals down, either on paper or on the computer. Committing them to memory is not an effective way to approach your time management system. Your brain can only remember so many things before it starts forgetting things. You want to be ready for your productivity sessions when they become available. You don't want to waste any of it trying to remember what you wanted to accomplish during that time.

5. **Confusing busyness with productivity**. When you are working on low-priority tasks, you are busy, but you aren't very productive. If a task is not high on your priority list, but you would rather do it than something that is on that list, you aren't progressing toward your goals. You are simply consuming your time with unproductive activities and putting off those that are going to move you forward.

6. **Not being flexible**. When you plan your day, your intentions are to stick to your schedule as much as possible. However, there will be times when you have to make unplanned changes to your schedule. This shouldn't be viewed as something that throws your time management plan into disarray, but rather as something that has a higher priority than what you had planned.

7. **Not understanding why you are doing your tasks**. Every task you put on your to-do list should move you closer to your goals. If you are engaged in an activity, but you don't know why you're spending time on it, you need to rethink that activity's importance in your life.

8. **Not setting realistic goals**. It can be easy to get carried away with your goals and make them too high, at least at first. Of course, you need those long-term goals, but your short-term goals should be realistic enough to allow you to progress toward your ultimate goals. Make your goals specific and measureable so you can track your progress along the way and determine when your goal has been met.

9. **Being unprepared**. You can only be productive if you are ready to get to work when time is available. This will help you get the most out of your 10 minute productivity sessions because you won't spend any time on preparation. You'll be able to dive right into the work.

10. **Trying to make everyone happy.** This mistake goes along with not being able to say no. Certainly, you want to help others when you can, but you need to keep yourself your highest priority. This might sound selfish, but it's a huge key to effective time management. You simply can't please all the people all the time.

Now that you are aware of these common mistakes in time management, you can take a few minutes each day to make sure you aren't making them. Again, keep your reflection to less than 10 minutes to get the most out of your time. If you discover a mistake, take the necessary steps to correct it quickly so it doesn't lure you back into old habits.

Conclusion

The key to better time management is to create a plan and stick to it. This book has given you many 10 minute strategies to create your own time management plan that can easily fit into your life. Time management doesn't have to be complicated. With a little dedication and a lot of persistence, you can get your life back under control and have more time to do the things you really want to do.

Thank you again for purchasing this book!

I hope it was able to help you to manage your time effectively in 10 minutes or less.

The next step is to put the strategies and tips into practice and start finding more time to get things done without all the stress.

Finally, if you enjoyed this book, please take the time to share your thoughts and post a review on Amazon. It'd be greatly appreciated!

Thank you and good luck!

Ric Thompson

Please leave a review and let us know what you liked about this book by going to

https://www.amazon.com/gp/css/order-history

then clicking on Orders.

Check out this other Title by
Ric Thompson…

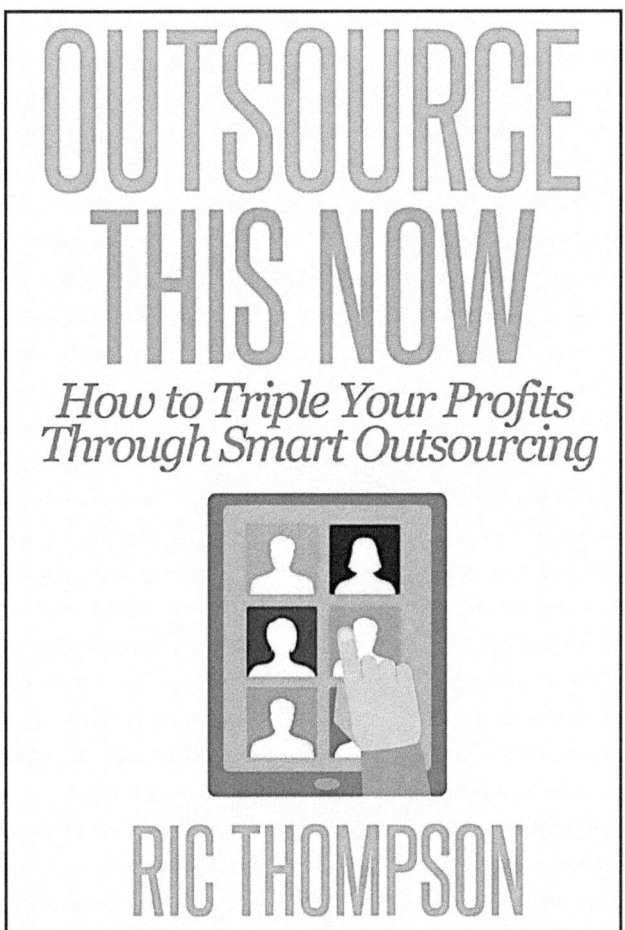

Outsource This Now

http://www.amazon.com/dp/B00H4HHY56

www.ingramcontent.com/pod-product-compliance
Lightning Source LLC
Chambersburg PA
CBHW071646170526
45166CB00003B/1461